Funny Food

made easy

Creative, Fun, & Healthy Breakfasts, Lunches, & Snacks

Funny Food
made easy

Bill & Claire Wurtzel • welcome BOOKS

This book is in honor of our mothers,
Beatrice Wurtzel and Anna Daniels.
We were both fortunate to have moms
who nourished us with love, food, and a
sense of playfulness. They showed us,
by example, how to find fun and joy in life.
This book is not only for children
but also for adults to enjoy making
whimsical art with healthy food.

•   •   •

Welcome Books®
An imprint of Rizzoli International Publications, Inc.
300 Park Avenue South
New York, NY 10010
www.rizzoliusa.com

Book Designer: Lori S. Malkin
Associate Publisher: James Muschett
Project Editor: Candice Fehrman

2016 2017 2018 2019 / 10 9 8 7 6 5 4 3 2 1

Printed in China

ISBN-13: 978-1-59962-133-3

Library of Congress Catalog Control Number: 2015951933

Workshops

FUNNY FOOD WORKSHOPS

We hope parents and teachers will use this book as a playful way to reinforce the importance of eating nourishing food and building good eating habits. Perhaps for your child's next birthday you'll throw a funny food party!

We began doing workshops for children after reading the statistics on the growing rate of childhood obesity and its long-term effects: type 2 diabetes, high blood pressure, and other diseases. In these creative workshops, families are introduced to the concept of a balanced diet as based on the U.S. Department of Health Guidelines for combining the five food groups.

The goal of these workshops is to entice kids and families to eat more fresh fruits and vegetables, whole grains, and low-fat dairy. We make it fun for kids and their families to learn about nutrition.

National Core Arts Standards released in October 2014 emphasize the importance of developing artistic ideas, refining them, and following them through to completion. A funny food workshop, in addition to being nutritious, is art instruction that fosters creativity.

This chapter explores how you can do workshops, too, and how you can encourage kids to try foods they have never tried before.

We hope the book will inspire you to make artistic, healthy food and discover the creativity that's in all of us.

ADULTS CAN PLAY TOO

Research on animals shows that mammals play automatically—just for the joy of it. They also learn about the social hierarchy and friendships through play. Adults may fear looking foolish or think playfulness is silly or frivolous. But according to Dr. Stuart Brown, a researcher and psychiatrist, "Play in childhood makes us happy, smart adults—and keeping it up can make us smarter at any age." In a TED Talk, Brown mentioned how play dramatically increases the rate of innovation in work groups. Play is fun and releases a chemical called dopamine that gives us pleasure, and that pleasure feeds the creative process. Re-engage the childlike sense of wonder and curiosity. Everyone wants to be around playful people.

Examine Your Mindset: Some people won't engage in certain play because they are afraid to take risks. They feel safe doing an activity where success is almost guaranteed. An inner voice tells them not to try. Attempt another mindset, one that sees growth coming from trying new things. Creative thinking is a skill that can be learned and developed in life.

Make Time for Play: Take time to engage in an activity like edible food play, and focus your senses on creating an imaginative plate. It is a great way to relieve stress and make time for playfulness. If you are a parent or teacher, your children or students will see that you are attending to your food, and they will want to do it too.

This book encourages people to take something familiar and make it strange. Forget that you're looking at a cantaloupe. Use the nonverbal part of your brain. Look at it as if for the first time. Wonder about it. Can you be surprised by what you create with this object, or can you surprise another person?

Find the child within you and enjoy the activity with delight.

"In every real man a child is hidden that wants to play."
— FRIEDRICH NIETZSCHE

PLAN AND STRUCTURE: DO YOUR

You don't need Bill to have your own funny food nutritious workshop. With a copy of this book and a variety of healthy ingredients, you can have fun with your child or groups of children.

Preparation

• An art teacher or a parent who is comfortable playing with food and can create a friendly atmosphere should take the lead. Select someone who gives children the freedom to make a nonrepresentational plate instead of a realistic image.

• Invite parents to attend.

• Use parent organizations to purchase food.

• Get a local supermarket to sponsor the workshop in exchange for free advertising. Buy nourishing food using as many food groups as possible. Focusing on fruits and vegetables is a MUST! Select fruits and vegetables in a variety of colors.

• Choose some foods from countries familiar to the group.

• Include some large fruits, such as apples, that can be sliced round (for heads and bodies) or even in strips (for arms and legs).

OWN FUNNY FOOD WORKSHOP

- Create a short pre-assessment to learn kids' baseline knowledge of food groups and healthy foods.

- Also do a post-assessment as a check for new knowledge. Both assessments can simply be informal chats.

- Stock up on this equipment: solid-color nine-inch paper plates, plastic knives, spoons, paper towels, bowls for cut-up veggies and berries, and hand sanitizer (if a sink is not available).

Presentation of Ingredients

- Wash and cut all the food.

- Separate ingredients into food groups and label them. Labels help children to recall the names.

- Children select food from a central table, or each table receives its own ingredients. If each table gets food, wait until after the slide show to distribute.

The Workshop Begins

- Show images from the book to captivate the group.

• Include photos of food groups and their importance in a balanced meal.

• Share simple facts, such as dairy (milk, yogurt, and cheese) builds strong bones and helps our muscles move, or fruits keep us from getting sick.

• Make a food plate or show a step-by-step illustration from the book.

Kids Make It and Eat It

• Encourage kids to make whatever they want—an imaginary creature, a pattern, a face, or an animal. Give them the freedom to make a one-eyed creature if that's what they want.

• Compliment the kids as they work: "The parsley makes great trees," or, "You thought to cut the strawberry in half for the lips," or, "I've never seen clementine ribs before."

• Guide children only if they have trouble and ask for help.

• Ask them to describe something about the healthy food on their plate, for example, "I used two different colored vegetables," or "I used all five food groups."

• Take photos of the creations before the kids begin to eat. Photos are great to display on bulletin boards, to

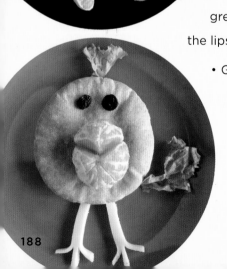

send home to the kids' families, and to give to the sponsoring supermarket.

• Children will gobble up what they make, discovering that healthy foods can be delicious. They will eat lettuce eyebrows, spinach hair, or a carrot nose if they make it.

. . .

Offer nutrition tips informally—at "just right" moments—and kids are more likely to remember them. There are many tips to choose from in this book.

. . .

For Young Children

With young children—four- and five-year-olds—you might want to focus the workshop on fruits.

• Show images made from fruits. The children will have fun identifying what the food portrays and the fruit used to make the image.

• Mention how important it is to eat fruit. Tell them that fruits of various colors have different nutrients that their bodies need to keep them strong.

• Introduce words related to their senses—squishy, sticky, juicy, soft, and fuzzy.

Table of
CONTENTS

Acknowledgments

We thank our daughters, Lisa and Nina, and our grandchildren, Ethan, Simon, and Daniela, for putting up with Bill's whacky dishes, for their participation in workshops, for their own funny food creations and, most of all, for enjoying healthy food. Thanks to James O. Muschett, our publisher, for his enthusiasm for our work and his guidance. Thanks to Lori S. Malkin for her creativity and hard work. And thanks to Candice Fehrman for her sharp eye in editing the book. We'd like to acknowledge Lena Tabori, the publisher of our first book, *Funny Food*, who supported us from the start. We offer our gratitude to friends and family who contributed their ideas for this book. We appreciate all the participants in our workshops who laughed, played, ate, and gave us important feedback.

I started making artistic breakfasts more than 50 years ago just to amuse Claire. They still make her smile. Food play was also a sneaky way to get our young kids and then grandkids to eat right. During all those years, my art was eaten, never to be seen again. A few years ago, I began photographing my plates. So now I can share how I create healthy breakfasts, snacks, and lunches. I hope this book inspires you to play with your food and have as much fun as I do. — BILL WURTZEL

INTRODUCTION

Hi!

Bill was an award-winning creative director in advertising for more than 30 years before switching to a career as a jazz guitarist. He is an avid improviser, and life with him is full of surprises. He likes to start his day by making breakfast for me. He's an artist—not just a cook. Bill's artistic eye plays a role, and fresh insights appear in the same familiar foods—a strawberry becomes a dinosaur or a steering wheel on a bus. Bill's spontaneous creations made with a few healthy ingredients stir my emotions, and his playfulness makes me feel happy and well nourished.

Our first book, *Funny Food*, was an unexpected adventure—filled with photos of healthy, whimsical breakfasts Bill had made for me. It was selected as a "best children's book of 2012" by the Bank Street College Children's Book Committee, and is now in its second printing.

We've had many requests for another book with more instructions and expanded meal suggestions. Our first book was a breakfast "look book." This sequel—*Funny Food Made Easy*—is a how-to book with easy step-by-step illustrations for making wholesome snacks, lunches, and more healthy breakfasts.

These are not sweet smiley-face sandwiches or little mouse-ear pancakes. These pages are filled with quirky images—a ridiculous yogurt elephant, an apple lion in cereal, and a pita portrait that looks like your neighbor. The

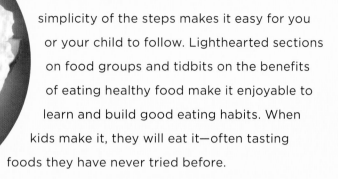

simplicity of the steps makes it easy for you or your child to follow. Lighthearted sections on food groups and tidbits on the benefits of eating healthy food make it enjoyable to learn and build good eating habits. When kids make it, they will eat it—often tasting foods they have never tried before.

We hope parents will use this book in a playful way to reinforce the importance of eating nourishing food. Perhaps you'll make your child's next birthday a funny food party for a wholesome celebration. Or take the book to your child's teacher—or the school's parent organization—so more children can participate in the fun and try new nutritious foods. Or look at the details for doing a workshop for a group of children.

The book is not just for children, though. A friend said she often gives the book as a hostess gift and "It makes a bigger splash than a bottle of wine." Just like kids, adults are drawn to the artistic images. They can enjoy the book merely as an entertaining art book, or use it as a guide to make funny food for their loved ones.

I hope this book will inspire you to make humorous healthy food. Making funny food for someone you love is fun and opens creative possibilities that you may not even know you have. — CLAIRE WURTZEL

THE ART OF FUNNY FOOD

Make funny food just for the fun of it. Since it's going to be eaten, it doesn't need to be a masterpiece. I do mostly breakfasts, lunches, and snacks, but an occasional dinner begs to be a funny food. I work quickly, usually within five minutes. That way, hot food stays hot, hunger is satiated, and creativity is fresh because there's not time to think too much.

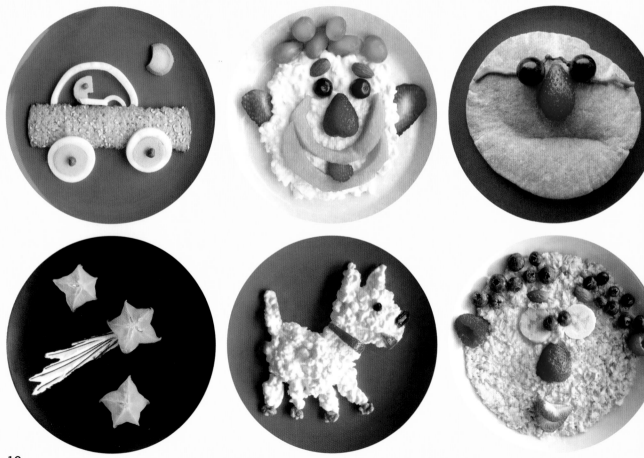

I use only fresh ingredients—lots of fruits and vegetables and low-fat and low-salt foods. I also always consider portion size.

Tools: Paring knife (plastic for young children) and a cutting board

Plates and Bowls: Plain white and assorted colors

Photos: Point-and-shoot or phone camera with natural light

"Every block of stone has a statue inside and it is the task of the sculptor to discover it." — MICHELANGELO

Choose Your Favorite Way of Working

Follow the Step-by-Step Photos: The ingredients don't have to be the same; use whatever you have available. If my plate shows a blueberry, you can substitute a raisin.

Imitate: Feel free to copy my work . . . not exactly, just as inspiration for your own choice of ingredients. Soon you'll catch on to my tricks.

Sketch: If you like to plan ahead, scribble out what you have in mind. It's only a guide and you can change your food art as you make it.

Be Spontaneous: I like working this way the most. Take risks. Focus on the food and see what you can come up with. If you use your imagination and follow your instinct, a cantaloupe and cherries may turn out to be a face with glasses.

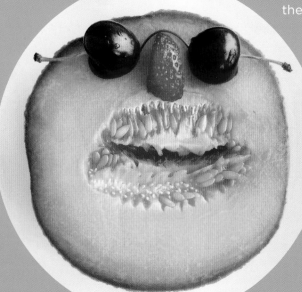

What Should I Make?

Anything!

Follow your heart and just have fun.

Be a Creative Devil

Focus on the food in front of you and let your creative juices flow. With a playful mind and a little imagination, see how many different ideas you can create from the same ingredients.

Take Risks

The happy accidents that might happen can lead to some unexpected and joyful creative ideas. If not, the food will be eaten or discarded anyway, so try something first. The mistakes show that you took a risk, let go, and played. Don't let fear get in your way—surrender to the process. The mistakes may lead to a moment of insight and delight that gives you a rush of energy.

"Capitalize on mistakes. Don't hide them—look at the mistake as an opportunity to rethink what's in front of you."

Festive Funny Food

Whether it's New Year's Day, Graduation Day, or Christmas, there's always a festive reason to celebrate with funny food. Try out your creativity on a holiday or other special day, like a birthday, for someone you know. It's fun for the entire family, and friends too!

New Year's Day

Super Bowl Sunday

Valentine's Day

Presidents' Day

Father's Day

Graduation Day

Memorial Day or Independence Day

18

St. Patrick's Day

Easter

Passover

Mother's Day

Columbus Day

Thanksgiving

Christmas

Halloween

Hanukkah

ACCIDENTS AND THE CREATIVE PROCESS

Bill has been creating hilarious, artistic food for more than 50 years—for me and our children and our grandchildren. We all love when Bill makes something unexpected.

Bill likes to set a restriction or rule for himself to use whatever is in the refrigerator or on the counter. He doesn't shop specifically for making funny food. On the other hand, he has a trained eye and will often select a bagel that has a natural mouth or cherries that have odd shapes.

An accidental burnt egg inspired this smiling creation.

When Bill makes a meal for me, he's fully engaged and loses a sense of time. It seems almost contradictory—he is serious and playful at the same time. He is laser focused on what he is making but also loose, silly, and imaginative.

Bill likes to begin his day in a quiet way. He asks what I want for breakfast and then I stay out of his way. Making his whacky, edible images is a nonverbal

"Build on observing things like a smiling egg, torn bread, a face in an apple or cheese . . . be open to surprises."

experience. He looks at the ingredients he has assembled and gets into the "flow"—lost in the moment of creating.

Accidents can be exhilarating. One afternoon, Bill sliced a pear for a snack. I saw his expression change when he looked at the sliced pear. By accident, the part of the dark seeds' coating got sliced off and Bill saw a cat's eyes. He was thrilled and presented me with the beautiful

This accidental face happened when pouring a bowl of vegetable-rich soup.

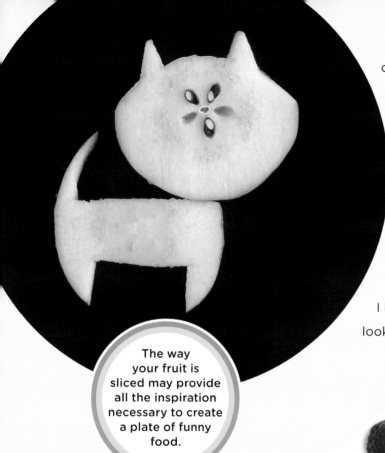

cat. The accident became an opportunity for a new creation. The pleasure of these surprise experiences inspires Bill to continue making this fantastic edible art. He says the joy comes from the unknown. He does it for the heck of it and then surprises himself. My role is to be his muse. I love his sensibility and always look forward to what's to come.

— CLAIRE WURTZEL

The way your fruit is sliced may provide all the inspiration necessary to create a plate of funny food.

"With an artist's palette consisting of whatever healthy food is on hand, I strive for a visual that will stir an emotion . . . ideally, a smile."

Breakfast

25

MAKE A **YOGURT** FACE WITH **OATMEAL** HAIR, RAISIN EYES, AND AN ALMOND NOSE. • TURN A **WHOLE-GRAIN PANCAKE** INTO A CAT WITH BIG BLUEBERRY EYES AND WALNUT FEET. •

BREAKFAST

Breakfast is the most important meal of the day. Turn your protein and grains into a comical healthy breakfast and you will get the nutrients you need for your physical strength and concentration.

• • •

Skipping breakfast puts your body in starvation mode, which is not good for your body or brain. People who don't eat breakfast tend to eat more throughout the day.

• • •

Follow one of the step-by-step breakfasts in this chapter, or use your imagination to inspire your own whacky meal.

WHAT TO EAT FOR BREAKFAST

Eggs are an excellent low-calorie protein food. You can make many different edible art plates with eggs: a hard-boiled egg caterpillar, a muffin face with scrambled egg curls, or a fried egg face with a yolk nose. Yogurt, a good source of dairy and protein, is also wonderful for making animals and people.

Adding fruit or nuts to yogurt, cereal, waffles, French toast, or pancakes cuts down on the need for sugar or syrup— an important health goal.

Look out for facial features in food. The holes in this cheese make perfect eyes for this bagel treat.

Parsilly

*Bagel, cream cheese, blueberries, cherry tomatoes,
white onion, parsley, smoked salmon*

Minnie

*Bagel, tomato, swiss cheese,
olives, smoked salmon*

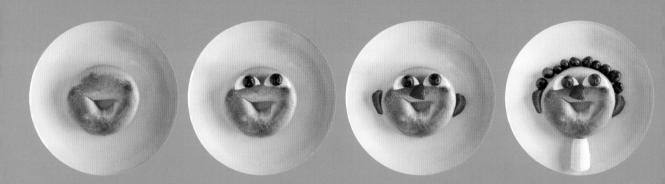

Berryo

Bagel, cheese, blueberries, strawberry, banana

Try choosing bagels with unusual holes, varied shades of brown, or a variety of seeds. Bill delights in taking something familiar and making it into something new. He surprises himself when a tight-lipped man, toothless lady, or romantic couple appears.

Soccerino

Bagel, hard-boiled egg, olives, grape tomato

Bagelspecs

Bagel, cream cheese, olives, grape tomato, red onion

31

Loxy

Bagel, smoked salmon, cream cheese, olives, parsley, cherry tomato, swiss cheese

Bagelmouth

Fried egg, strawberry, olives, bagel, parsley

Stubble

Fried egg, olives, bagel, basil, grape tomato, cheddar cheese, parsley, smoked salmon (or turkey or mushroom)

HAVE FUN!
Play with different ingredients until you find a design you like.

33

Cooking Eggs

Eggs are a nutritious miracle. They are one of the highest-quality proteins found in any food—they contain all nine essential amino acids, are filled with vitamins, and have only 70 calories. And they're inexpensive.

An egg has an amazing ability to transform itself. Try it scrambled, poached, hard-boiled, soft-boiled, fried, or in an omelet. Eggs are usually best when cooked slowly.

New research shows that moderate consumption of eggs does not have a negative impact on cholesterol if you eat a well-balanced low-fat and low-cholesterol diet. Don't skip the yolks; they contain most of the egg's vitamin supply.

Fry: Heat a medium skillet, preferably nonstick, over medium-low heat for about a minute, add a pat of butter (or olive oil spray), and swirl it around the pan. Add the cracked eggs to the skillet. Turn the heat to low. Some people cover the pan for 30 seconds. Or, as soon as the whites are firm, in about a minute, remove the eggs from the pan and serve.

Scramble: Place a medium skillet over medium heat for about a minute. Add butter or olive oil spray and swirl it around the pan. Meanwhile, crack the eggs into a bowl and beat them until the yolks and whites are uniform in color. Beat in one or two tablespoons of milk, add the mixture to the skillet, and turn the heat to medium low. Cook, stirring frequently, until the eggs are no longer runny (two to three minutes) and serve.

"Any way you eat them— eggs are eggs-ellent!"

Hard-boil: Place the eggs in a pan with enough cold water to cover them, being careful not to crowd them. Turn the heat on medium low. When the water begins to boil, reduce the heat to low and cover the pan. Gently boil for 10 minutes. To remove the shell, plunge the egg into cold running water and then peel and serve.

Soft-boil: Place the eggs in a pan with enough cold water to cover them, being careful not to crowd them. Turn the heat on medium low. When the water begins to boil, reduce the heat to low and gently boil for three or four minutes. Run the egg under cold water before cracking the shell to scoop out the egg.

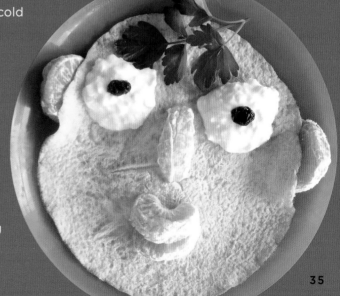

TAKE A FEW STANDARD INGREDIENTS—SUNNY-SIDE-UP EGGS, BREAD, VEGETABLES, FRUIT, AND CHEESE—AND HAVE FUN WITH ALL THE VARIATIONS YOU CAN CREATE.

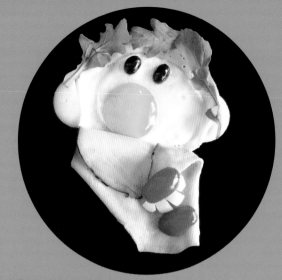

Pepperlips *Fried egg, parsley, lettuce, mushrooms, carrot, red pepper, olives*

Hamanegg *Fried egg, ham, grape tomatoes, olives, lettuce, cheese*

Dilly Billy *Fried egg, smoked salmon, grape tomato, red onion, basil, dill, olives, bread*

Hattie
Fried egg, bread, arugula, strawberry, raisins

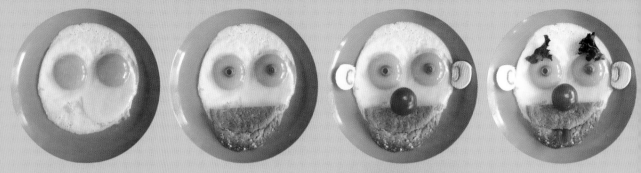

Sunny

*Fried egg, bread,
olives, mushrooms,
cherry tomato, lettuce*

Bill really doesn't
know what's going to
materialize when he
starts making a dish.
He simply uses whatever
ingredients are at hand.
Nothing is wasted. Surprise
yourself and watch a bread
heel become a mouth!

Chivy
Fried egg, chives, olives, cherry tomato, carrots

Yolknose
Fried egg, olives, ham, cheese, lettuce, bread, grape tomato

39

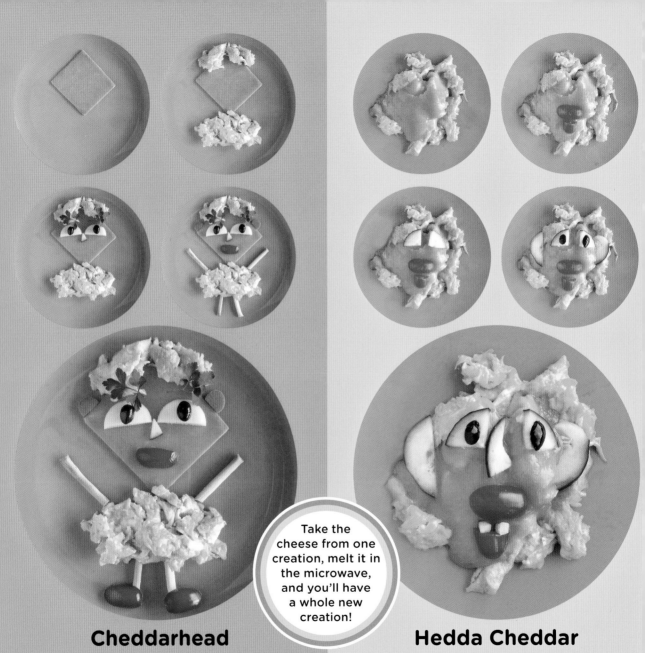

Take the cheese from one creation, melt it in the microwave, and you'll have a whole new creation!

Cheddarhead

Cheese, scrambled egg, parsley, olives, cucumber, carrot, grape tomatoes, breadsticks

Hedda Cheddar

Scrambled egg, cheese, grape tomato, cucumber, olives

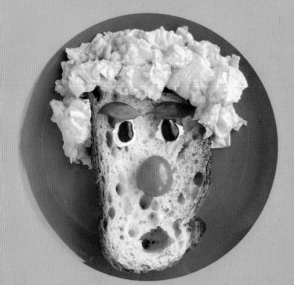

Holeo *Scrambled egg, bread, cherry tomato, basil, olives, cream cheese*

Snappy
Egg, cucumber, olive

Chivey Chick *Scrambled egg, swiss cheese, olives, basil, chives*

Cakeface *Scrambled egg, cheese, orange, banana, blueberry (halved), rice cake*

V
A
R
I
A
T
I
O
N
S

41

Brocco

Egg, cottage cheese, olives, broccoli, grape tomato, cucumber, basil, carrot

Egghead

Egg, toast, carrot, olives, parsley, cucumber, grape tomato

Yellow Fellow

Egg, cottage cheese, blueberries, strawberry, parsley

43

"I have learned
throughout
my life as
a composer
chiefly through
my mistakes."
— IGOR STRAVINSKY

44

FLAT EGGS:
Egg Beaters—made with real eggs—are an alternative to shell eggs. They have half the calories of shell eggs, provide the same protein, and make easy "flat" scrambled eggs.

45

Use your imagination.

An egg slicer gives you the shapes to transform a lowly hard-boiled egg into "eggs-otic" creatures.

Anything is possible!

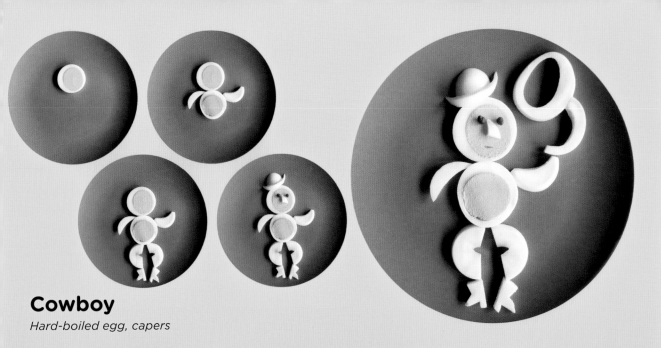

Cowboy
Hard-boiled egg, capers

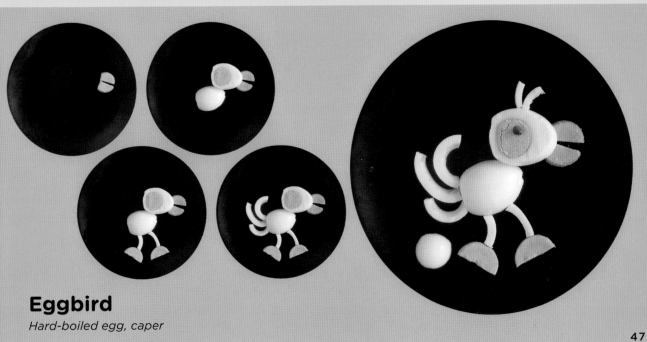

Eggbird
Hard-boiled egg, caper

47

RAISIN BREAD •
MULTIGRAIN LOAF •
ENGLISH MUFFINS •
WHOLE-WHEAT BREAD •
RYE BREAD •
PUMPERNICKEL •
TOAST •
BAGUETTE •
MATZOH •
FRENCH TOAST •

Breadie

Bread, strawberry, blueberries, parsley

Sy Clops

*Fried egg, olive, bread, cheese,
cherry tomato, chives*

49

Wholewheaty
Bread, strawberry, blueberries

Buttons
Bread, hard-boiled egg, olives, parsley

Cherrynose
Bread, cherries, hard-boiled egg, blueberries

Breadheart *Bread, banana, blueberries, almonds, raspberry, strawberry*

V A R I A T I O N S

Play with an Animal

Mammals play for the joy of it. It also prepares them for the unexpected. Kids especially love animals.

> When children are actively engaged in exploring with their food, they are planting the seeds for a healthy lifestyle.

They love to look at Bill's animal-themed plates, and then make and eat their own. Sometimes they become the animals, mimicking their sounds. Making animal dishes is a great way to get kids to eat a hearty meal.

Breadmobile

Bread, hard-boiled egg, olive, parsley, carrot

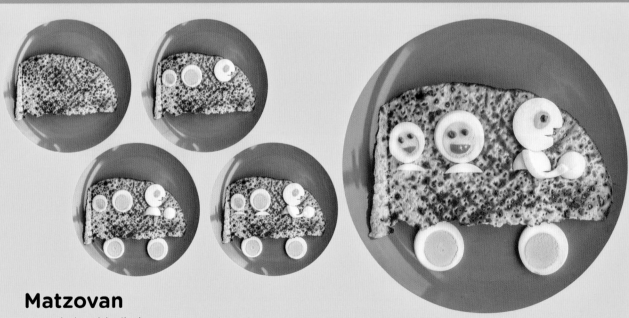

Matzovan

Matzoh, hard-boiled egg, capers, tomato

Play with Shapes!

Experiment with cutting foods in unexpected shapes to make funny faces. Bill's silly portraits often remind us of ourselves—in spirit if not in looks.

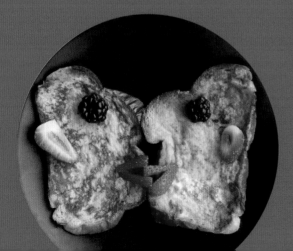

Food play can be family fun!

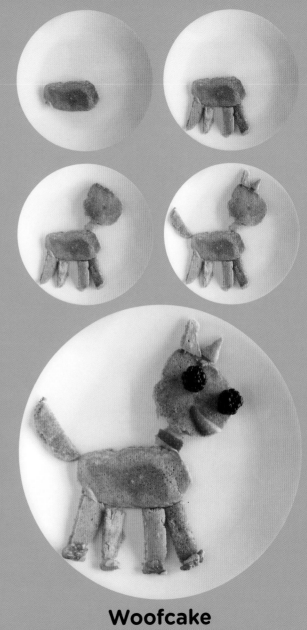

Woofcake
Pancake, blackberries, strawberry, walnuts

Monkeycake

Pancake, banana, raisins

Teddycake

Pancake, strawberry, raspberry, cashews, blueberries

56

Mousecake
Pancake, cottage cheese, blueberries

Be Silly!

Poopcake *Pancake, strawberry, blueberries, cashews, almonds, walnut*

Billy Cake *Pancake, banana, lettuce, melon, strawberry, blueberries, walnuts, powdered sugar*

Goofycake
Pancake, banana, raisins, walnuts

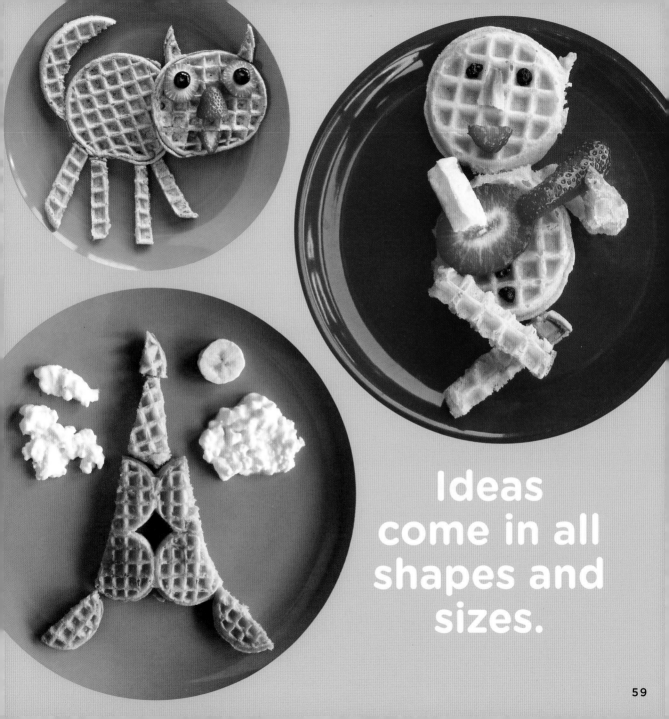

Ideas come in all shapes and sizes.

Waffo

Waffle, strawberry, raspberry, blueberries, cheese, banana, parsley

Waffly

Waffle, cheese, blueberries, breakfast sausage, strawberry, clementine, parsley

Nananose

*Oatmeal, banana, blueberries,
clementine, pecans*

A great way to start the day
is with steel-cut oatmeal.
Steel-cut oats are whole
grains that take time
to cook, about 25
minutes. Cut the
cooking time in half
with an easy shortcut:
for four servings, boil
four cups of water
and then add one cup
of oats and simmer for
one minute. Turn off the
heat, cover the pot, and store
overnight in the refrigerator. In
the morning, heat the oatmeal until
it's tender, about 10 minutes.

Save
leftover cooked
oatmeal for another
morning, heating
it with low-fat milk
for added protein
and creaminess.

"Creative thinking is a skill that can be learned and developed in life."

Mighty Oat

Apple, oatmeal, raisins

Oatso *Oatmeal, strawberry, banana, blackberries, cottage cheese, parsley*

Yogoat
Oatmeal, yogurt, almond, raisins

Smileyoat
Oatmeal, blueberries, banana

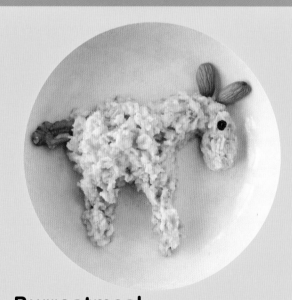

Burroatmeal
Oatmeal, almonds, walnut, raisin

V
A
R
I
A
T
I
O
N
S

BLACKBERRIES • APPLES • CHEERIOS • STRAWBERRIES • SHREDDED WHEAT • BANANAS • BRAN • CORNFLAKES • PEACHES • BLUEBERRIES • PLUMS • CHEX • NUTS • RAISIN BRAN

65

Flakey

Cornflakes, banana, blueberries, strawberry, cashews

Breakfast cereal is quick and easy. Whole-grain, low-sugar cereals are the healthiest, easiest to digest, and keep you feeling full longer. Check labels for sugar and fat content. Avoid high-fructose corn syrup, which is processed and not a healthy way to start the day. Add low-fat milk or yogurt, fresh fruit, raisins, or nuts for added flavor and you're on your way to meeting your daily nutritional needs.

Whole-grain cereals are a good source of soluble fiber, which acts almost like a sponge, sucking up bad (LDL) cholesterol in your body.

Cattage Cheese

*Cottage cheese, banana, strawberry,
blueberries, cashews, English muffin*

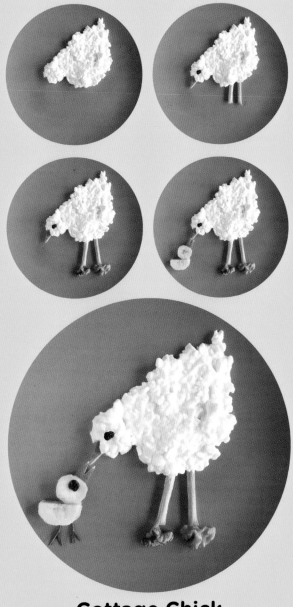

Cottage Chick

*Cottage cheese, breadsticks, raisins, apple,
walnuts, banana, chives*

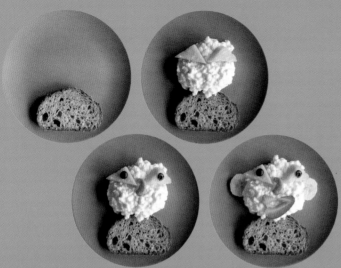

Buttony

Bread, cottage cheese, pineapple, blueberries, cashew, strawberry, banana, raspberries

Berryface

Cottage cheese, strawberries

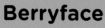

Cherry Balloon
Cottage cheese, peach, cherry, blueberries

Cottage Trees
Cottage cheese, banana

V
A
R
I
A
T
I
O
N
S

Cinnamatic *Cottage cheese, banana, cantaloupe, strawberry, blueberries, cinnamon*

Fruiticia *Cottage cheese, strawberry, banana, grapes, blueberries, almonds*

69

Cottage cheese boosts your intake of calcium, vitamin A, and vitamin B5, which is good to reduce stress and helps your brain function better.

. . . and enjoy the activity with delight."

70

Spooning yogurt
or cottage cheese into
a measuring cup helps
you keep track of
amounts and gives you
a nice round shape to
work with.

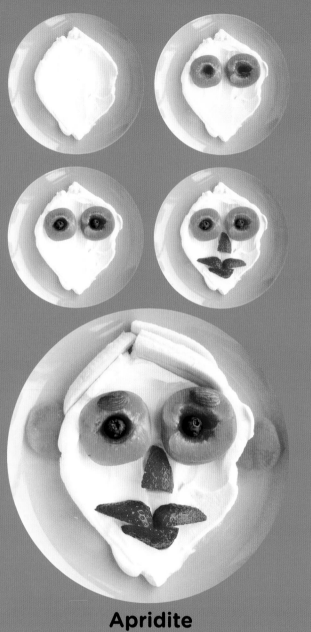

Apridite

*Yogurt, apricot, blueberries,
strawberry, banana, almonds*

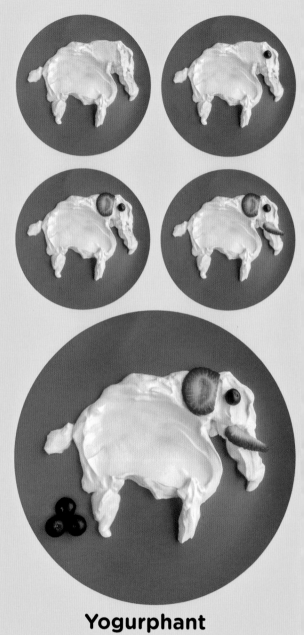

Yogurphant

Yogurt, blueberries, strawberry

72

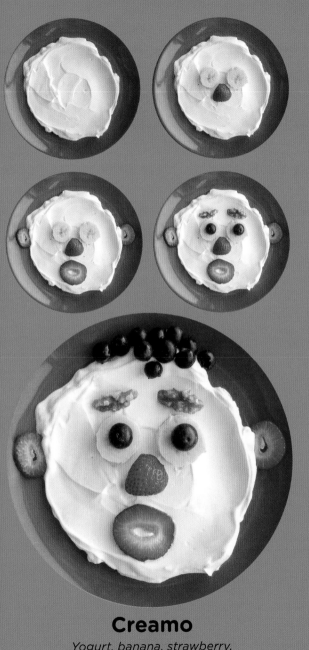

Creamo

*Yogurt, banana, strawberry,
blueberries, walnuts*

Redcap

Yogurt, blueberry, strawberry, almonds

73

"Stay open, don't label what it is, and practice. Practice helps us be able to express what we feel and unblock the natural flow . . .

. . .With practice, it is easier to become spontaneous."

To prevent any round food, such as berries, from rolling, cut them in half.

76

Snacks

MAKE PEOPLE, PLANES, AND PENGUINS. •CREATE BIRDS, BEES, AND BUSES. •TURN FRUIT INTO FISH, FARM ANIMALS, AND FLYING MACHINES. BUILD CASTLES MADE OF CRACKERS. •

SNACKS

People who eat wholesome snacks eat less at meals. Eating smaller amounts of food more frequently keeps your metabolism revved up.

• • •

Children need nutritious snacks between meals. Their growing bodies and developing brains need regular refueling.

• • •

Snacks give you an opportunity to get in some of your daily nutritional needs.

WHAT TO EAT FOR A SNACK

Fruit is a great snack, especially when you eat the actual fruit rather than just the juice of the fruit. Juicing strips out the fiber. You need fiber for good digestion and elimination. Other snacks—such as raw vegetables, air-popped popcorn, legumes, nuts, peanut butter on whole-grain crackers, and hummus—are also packed with fiber.

Low-fat yogurt, cottage cheese, and other low-fat cheese are also great snacks. They provide nourishing dairy and protein.

Grab-and-Go Snacks: Sliced carrots, bananas, clementines, apples, raisins, dried fruit, and nuts are satisfying and provide the nutrients your body needs. Individual bags of popcorn, fresh berries, cut-up watermelon, or individually wrapped cheese slices are other healthy and delicious snacks.

Yogurt and cottage cheese both come in single-serving containers for a grab-and-go snack.

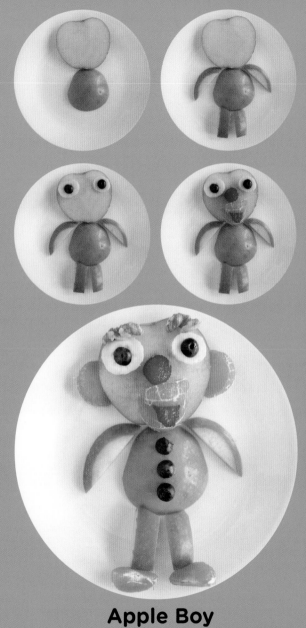

Apple Girl

*Apple, clementine,
cheese, raisins*

Apple Boy

*Apple, banana, blueberries, clementine,
raspberries, walnuts*

81

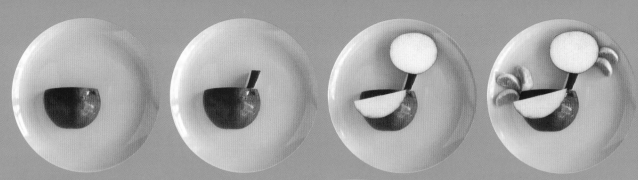

Apple Bird

Apple, clementine, raisin, cheese

The skin of an apple has more value than the flesh inside. Apples come in different colors and have lots of vitamins A and C, potassium, calcium, and iron.

Apples keep our bodies strong, and help our bodies fight against infections. Adding nuts and cheese to a fruit snack gives you an energy boost—and may also help your mood.

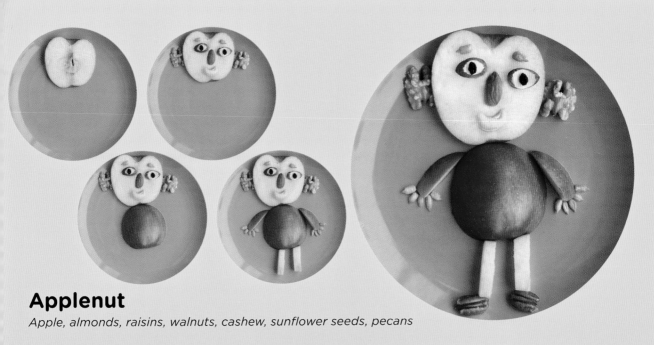

Applenut

Apple, almonds, raisins, walnuts, cashew, sunflower seeds, pecans

Appleo

Apple, carrots, crackers, cheese, raisins, parsley, clementine

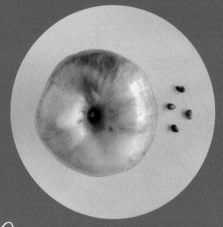

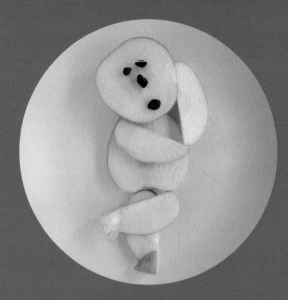

Simplicity

Making fun snack plates doesn't have to be complicated. With just four raisins and an apple, you can make countless different creations. Cut the apples into different shapes and play around with the arrangement. Do the same thing with a banana and you'll have a circle of friends on your plate.

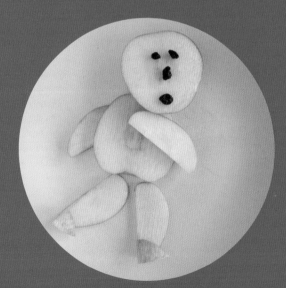

Be creative about how you cut the fruit. Slices don't need to be uniform, and you can cut pieces into any size or shape.

Pearpuss

Pear

Shakespear

Pear, raisins

Pearformer

Pear

Stradipearius

Pear

V A R I A T I O N S

In addition to plums, Bill shapes birds with grapes, pears, or apples.

Plumbird

Yogurt, plum, grapes

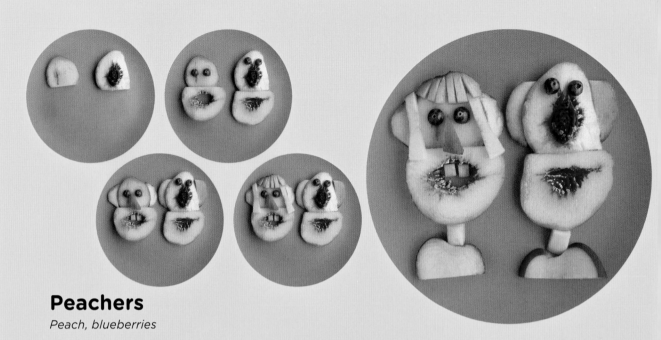

Peachers

Peach, blueberries

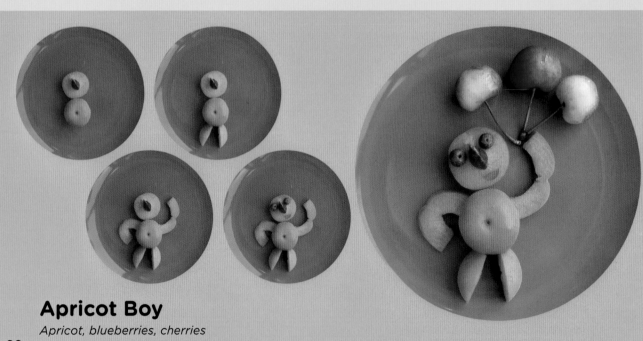

Apricot Boy

Apricot, blueberries, cherries

Peach Train
Peach, strawberry, waffle, blueberries, banana, breadstick

Peach Bee
Peach, plum, blueberries

V A R I A T I O N S

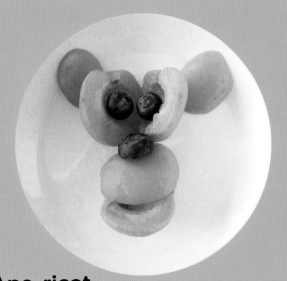

Ape-ricot
Apricot, blueberries

Apricoto
Apricot, English muffin, blueberries

89

Bananaboard

Banana, peanut butter, raisins,
strawberry, walnut

Bananas have a lot of calories, which give you energy. Have a banana if you feel tired or after exercising or playing. Bananas are easy to digest because they are so soft. They were probably the first fruit you ate as a baby. They are a good source of vitamin B6 for good strong blood, vitamin C to help fight infections, and minerals to help strengthen your bones.

Bananas are a great grab-and-go snack that doesn't have to be washed.

Banana Plane

Cottage cheese, banana, strawberries

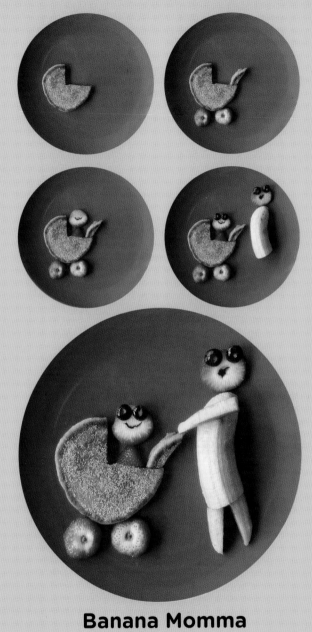

Banana Momma

English muffin, strawberries, blueberries, banana

91

Bananaraffe

Banana, walnuts, raisins, parsley

Bananaface
Banana, clementine

Banana Skater
Banana, strawberries

Banana Bath
Banana, blueberries, yogurt

Acrobananics
Banana

VARIATIONS

93

Sometimes Less is More

Bill often uses food to create the shape of a face.
Since faces are round like plates, though, you can
also just put on the features and you're good to go!

Berry Bird
Strawberries

Wildflower
Kiwi, strawberry, raspberries, parsley

95

EAT A RAINBOW OF DIFFERENT COLORS OF FRUITS AND VEGETABLES. • EACH COLOR HAS ITS OWN UNIQUE SET OF VITAMINS AND MINERALS TO KEEP YOU AND YOUR FAMILY HEALTHY. •

Mangola

Mango, raisins, dried cranberry

Clem

Clementine, blueberries

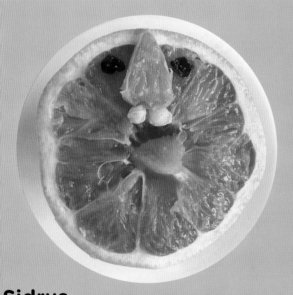

Sidrus

Grapefruit, raisins

Figgies

Fig, yogurt, raisins

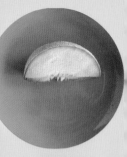

Freda

Cantaloupe, pineapple, blueberries, strawberry, blackberries, raspberries, cherries

Seedstache

Cantaloupe, blueberries

Crescent

*Cantaloupe, banana, blueberry,
strawberry, cottage cheese*

Cantaloupia

*Cantaloupe, blackberries, blueberries,
strawberry, raspberry*

99

One cup of watermelon has only 46 calories and is refreshing and filling. It is bursting with nutrients and is fat free and low in sodium—an ideal snack. Watermelon is a sweet, refreshing treat to add to a salad.

GET KIDS **PLAYING** WITH HEALTHY FOOD TO ENCOURAGE THEM TO EXPAND THEIR FOOD CHOICES. • **SHARING** TIPS ABOUT **NUTRITION** WHILE KIDS ARE ENGAGED IS THE IDEAL CONDITION FOR **LEARNING**. •

Pineapple is filled with surprises, starting with its prickly outside and sweet and juicy inside. Another surprise: it is made up of many berries that grow together around the central core.

. . . and keeping it up can make us smarter at any age." — DR. STUART BROWN

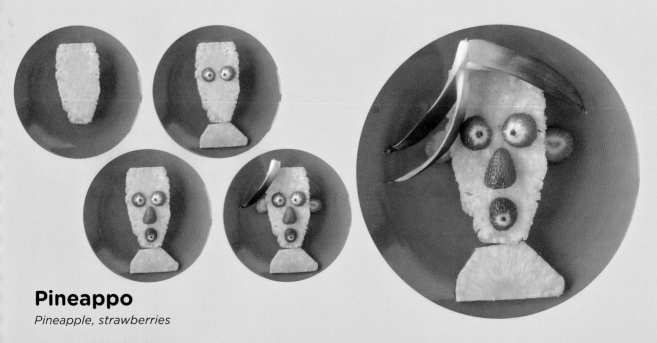

Pineappo
Pineapple, strawberries

Pinecone
Cottage cheese, waffle, pineapple, clementine, banana, blueberry

103

Dried Fruit: Dried fruit is simply fresh fruit with the water removed. Remember that the dried fruit is a fraction of the size of the fresh one, but has the same number of calories and the same amount of sugar. Don't let your eyes fool you! You can dry fruit at home in a sunny window and watch the grape morph into a raisin—much to your child's delight.

Nuts: For great creations and healthy, grab-and-go snacks, reach for nuts. You and your active child can both benefit from a handful of nuts. A handful is equal to a half-cup serving. Stick to a serving size to get the nuggets of nutrients while limiting the calories. Nuts are packed with protein, fiber, vitamin E, and a bundle of other vitamins and minerals.

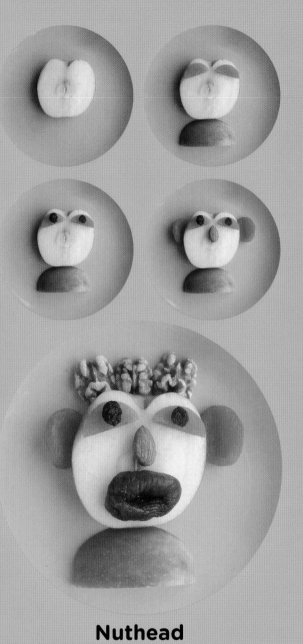

Nuthead

Apple, apricot, raisins, almond,
walnuts, fig

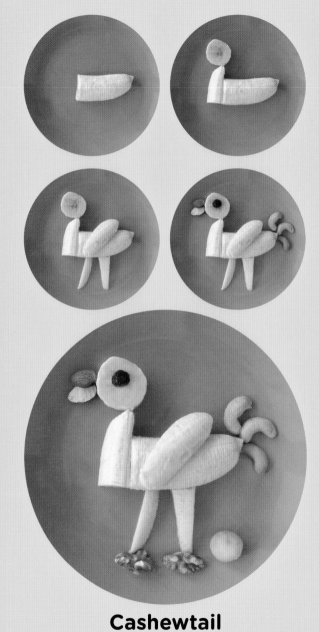

Cashewtail

Banana, raisin, almonds, cashews,
walnuts, macadamia nut

If kids make it, they'll eat it.

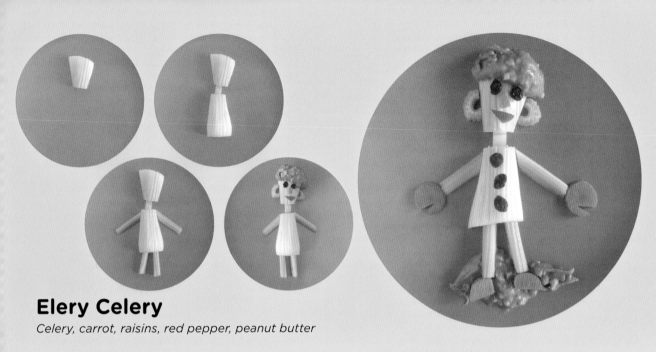

Elery Celery

Celery, carrot, raisins, red pepper, peanut butter

Melonlip

Lettuce, watermelon, clementine, walnut, pineapple, blueberries

Who Gets the Gold Star— Yogurt or Cottage Cheese?

Although both provide calcium and vitamin B12, there are differences. Low-fat yogurt delivers twice as much calcium as low-fat cottage cheese per serving, but the cottage cheese is higher in protein. Yogurt has fewer calories cup for cup. But cottage cheese has fewer carbs per serving than yogurt. Eat them both. They are versatile—they are great eaten alone or mixed in with other ingredients. Let your mood or your nutritional needs determine which one you grab.

Fetcher
Cheese, breadstick, raisins

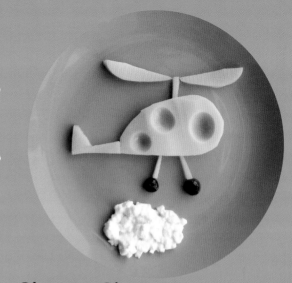

Cheese Chopper
Cheese, cottage cheese, blueberries

Cheese Ball
Cheese, lettuce, cherry tomato

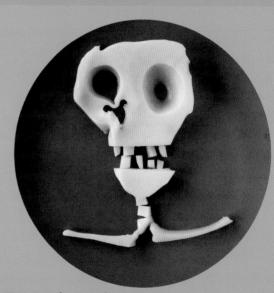

Bonehead
Cheese

VARIATIONS

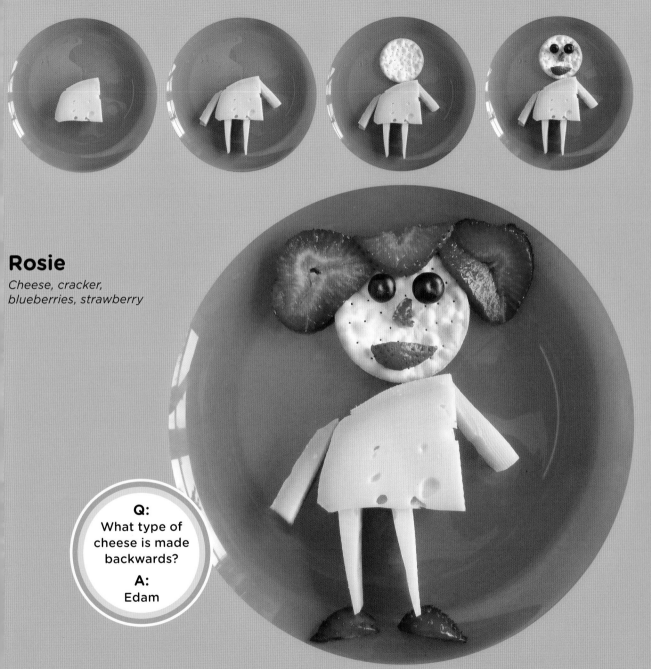

Rosie

Cheese, cracker, blueberries, strawberry

Q:
What type of cheese is made backwards?

A:
Edam

111

DID YOU KNOW?
Peanut butter is not actually made from nuts. Peanuts are legumes that grow underground; nuts grow on trees or shrubs.

Nutsy

English muffin, peanut butter, banana, raisins, almonds, apricot

Peanuto
Bagel, peanut butter, banana, almond, raisins

Skippy *Rice cake, peanut butter, walnuts, almonds, cashews, raisins*

Toasty
Toast, peanut butter, raisins, pomegranate seed

Spike
Bread, strawberry, banana, raisins, peanut butter

V
A
R
I
A
T
I
O
N
S

The Whole Whole-Grain Story!

Check ingredients. Almost every package says multigrain, bran, stone ground, or organic. That may sound healthy, but unless the package indicates that the product is whole grain, it is not. Whole grains are the healthiest grains, and can lower your risk of heart disease, diabetes, and other health problems. Get your kids to eat whole grains.

Peter Pita

*Pita, strawberry, clementine,
cheese, raisins, parsley*

Wheatly

*Cracker, cheese, olives, tomato,
lettuce, snow pea*

Cracker Towers

Crackers, Jarlsberg cheese rind, cheese, broccoli

Whole-wheat crackers can crack you up when you use them creatively. Besides broccoli, parsley, basil, and other leafy herbs make excellent trees.

Lunch

USE BROCCOLI TO MAKE HILARIOUS HAIR AND FUNNY NOSES. • OLIVES, PEAS, AND CAPERS MAKE GREAT EYES. • TASTY TOMATOES MAKE GREAT TONGUES, NOSES, EARS, AND MOUTHS.

LUNCH

Make time for a healthy lunch!
It reduces stress and renews your energy.

• • •

Unhealthy choices can sap your energy, upset your sleep pattern,
and affect your behavior.

• • •

Swap poor food choices for colorful fruits and vegetables,
whole grains, and protein and you'll feel it—in your
energy level and ability to focus.

WHAT TO EAT FOR LUNCH

Lentils or split peas in a soup or salad are good proteins and are among the best fiber foods. Leftover quinoa makes a great salad, and is a complete protein. It is one of the richest foods you can eat.

Whole-grain crackers or bread with hummus or tuna and some chopped vegetables and basil are yummy.

Cold wild salmon has the omega-3 fats that reduce the risk of heart attacks and strokes. Add nourishing ingredients to enrich a lunch salad: fruit, a hard-boiled egg, shaved parmesan cheese, an avocado, or pomegranate seeds are delicious and help meet the daily requirements of vitamins and minerals.

Make a soup with legumes, vegetables that have lost their freshness, onion, and some herbs, such as parsley or dill. The soup, along with hummus on whole-grain bread, makes a healthy lunch.

Kids may eat it if it has a surprise ingredient, like pomegranates, raspberries, or blueberries.

Hoagie

*Bread, turkey, tomato, lettuce, cheese,
cucumber, carrot, parsley, olives*

Pumpernicko

*Bread, turkey, basil, avocado,
olives, carrot, tomato*

123

Sam Wich

Bread, turkey, parsley, radish, olives, cheese

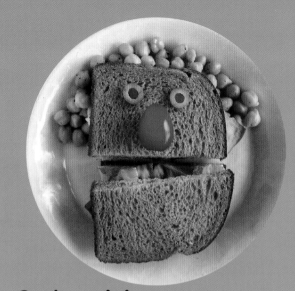

Garbonzini *Bread, turkey, garbanzo beans, olives, grape tomato, lettuce*

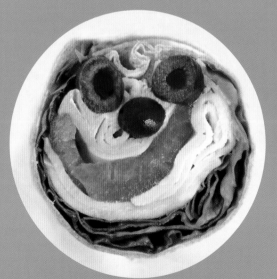

Wrappy

Tortilla, lettuce, turkey, tomato, olives

Rye Guy *Bread, cherry tomato, blueberries, cheese, arugula*

V
A
R
I
A
T
I
O
N
S

Sandy Wich *Bread, turkey, parsley, garbanzo beans, olives, tomato*

Shrimpstache *Bread, arugula, grape tomato, olives, garbanzo beans, shrimp*

"Mindset is probably the most important influence on our creative ability." — CAROL DWECK

Mozzarella Fellas
Bread, pesto, basil, tomato, mozzarella, olives

125

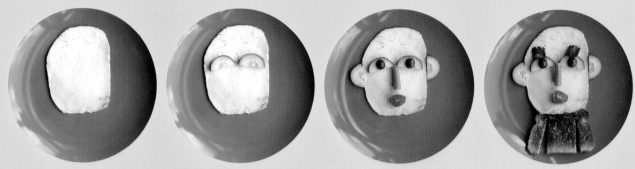

Tom Turkey

*Turkey, cucumber, olives,
carrot, cherry tomato, parsley,
black beans, cheese, bread*

Chicken or turkey breasts—grilled or broiled—make a few good meals. Cook them once and then have extra at the ready.

No time to cook? Buy low-fat sandwich meat from the grocery deli, sliced fresh. It's lower in sodium than prepackaged meat.

Low-fat cheese is a good source of calcium. It builds bones and keeps them strong. The nutrients in dairy include calcium, potassium, vitamin D, and protein. Don't swallow a pill. Studies show that it's healthier to eat foods that provide natural sources of calcium rather than taking calcium pills.

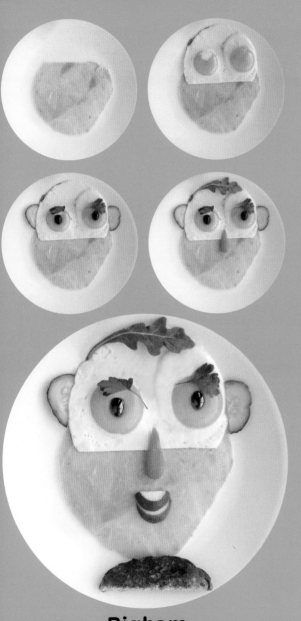

Bigham

Ham, fried egg, cucumber, arugula, olives, carrot, radish, bread

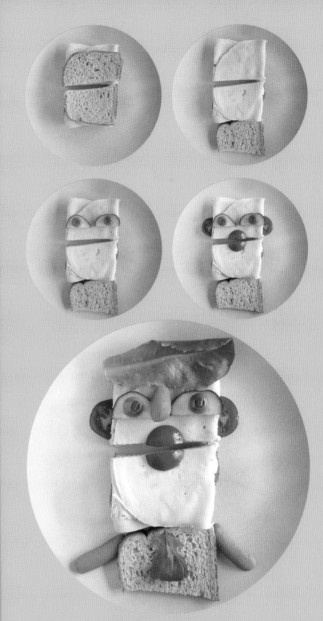

Talky Turkey

Bread, turkey, cucumber, olives, cherry tomato, lettuce, carrot

127

Be creative with deli orders—no holds barred! Holes in cheese can be eyes, nostrils, or freckles. Cheese is good for use as eyes or teeth. Use deli meat as a base for a face—folded, it puts a smile on your plate.

Baguetto

Baguette, cheese, olives, carrot, cucumber, tomato, basil

Grillo

Bread, cheese (white and yellow), tomato, basil, olives

Mozzie *Mozzarella cheese, English muffin, olives (black and green), tomato, carrot, cucumber, chives, basil, lettuce*

Rollo
Roll, cheese, grape tomato, raisins

131

V A R I A T I O N S

Eggster
Bread, hard-boiled egg, scrambed egg, capers

Egg Bouquet
Bread, parsley, hard-boiled egg, cherry tomatoes

Basilbrow *Bagel, hard-boiled egg, basil, parsley, tomato, olives*

Eggerina *Bread, hard-boiled egg, strawberry, blueberries, parsley*

Muffinigan

English muffin, hard-boiled egg, grape tomatoes, capers, lettuce

Sliced tomatoes make wonderful mouths because the seeds are perfect teeth. Try moving things around—tomato for ears and cheese or egg for a mouth. Mix it up and surprise yourself.

133

Burger Burt

Burger, bun, sweet potato fries, red onion, olives, pickle, tomato, lettuce

Making Healthy Burgers

• To make healthy burgers, use a combination of half lean ground beef and ground turkey. Or, for a less expensive meal with added flavor and lower fat, reduce the amount of beef and add a portion of grains, such as lentils or bulgur wheat.

• Fill half of your plate with veggies, and the other half with a combination of lean protein and whole grains. The vegetables are filling and each color provides a different range of vitamins and nutrients. Emphasize dark green vegetables like broccoli, kale, and spinach, but don't forget white vegetables like cauliflower, onions, potatoes, and turnips.

• The serving size of protein matters. As a basic rule, the size of your palm, not including the fingers, is the amount of protein you should eat. Or, use a deck of cards as your reference for a good-size portion.

Lively Leftovers

Chicken is low in fat, cooks quickly, and has a mild flavor. It tastes great with herbs or spices and vegetables. Chicken breasts cook in a couple of minutes—on the stove, under the broiler, in the oven, or in a wok. Leftover chicken makes hearty lunches.

Hot Chicken: Chop or slice and add to a soup; heat with leftover grains; or sauté with cut veggies.

Cold Chicken: Add fresh parsley to a chicken dish. It's a great source of vitamins A, C, K, and folate. Try some basil on a cold chicken sandwich, and add vitamins K, A, iron, and calcium to your diet. Spread pesto on whole-grain bread to augment chicken salad. Try plain yogurt or Greek tzatziki instead of mayo on cold chopped chicken. Cut grapes or walnuts to add nutrients and flavor. Another flavorful

Quinoa, with added chicken or fish, makes a great easy-to-go lunch.

boost for cold-sliced chicken is to put it in a "garden" of avocado, pomegranates, lettuce, tomatoes, and some shaved Parmesan cheese.

Batch Cooking: I cook once and have leftovers for multiple meals, or I freeze for when I want to concoct another meal. As long as you're cooking, double or triple the recipe. Keep leftover grains in the freezer and add to soups or defrost and add to a salad. Make oversize quantities of soup and freeze in portion sizes. Take it out in the morning, and it defrosts by lunchtime.

Hot Meals for Lunch: Heat up leftovers for a hearty hot lunch. Nurture yourself: take a meal to work that can easily be heated in the microwave. Send kids to school with a thermos of soup or other hearty leftovers. Add a frozen bottle of water to keep the food cold.

Luscious Lamb

Lamp chops are lean, if trimmed, and are an excellent source of protein. Eating four ounces of lamb also provides vitamin B12, niacin, and riboflavin. Rib chops are very tender, but shoulder chops are much less expensive and equally flavorful. Kids often enjoy lamb chops. Be careful that the dog doesn't grab the bone!

Sole Sister *Fish, sweet potato, grape tomato, hard-boiled egg, lettuce, olives*

Bluefish *Fish, kale, sweet potato, peas, red pepper, lemon, mushrooms*

Fishpants

Toast, fish, tomato, capers, lettuce

Try canned sardines—they are easy to open and filled with omega-3 fatty acids, minerals, and vitamins.

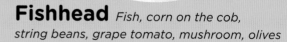

Fishhead *Fish, corn on the cob, string beans, grape tomato, mushroom, olives*

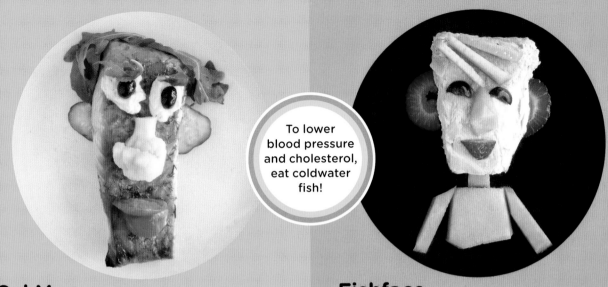

Sal Mon *Salmon, arugula, yogurt, olives, cucumber, cauliflower, tomato*

Fishface
Fish, blueberry (halved), melon, strawberry

To lower blood pressure and cholesterol, eat coldwater fish!

Eat Coldwater Fish for Strong Bones

Coldwater fish (tuna, salmon, herring, mackerel, and sardines) provide vitamin D, which aids calcium absorption and helps keep your bones strong. Eat one or two servings of fatty, coldwater fish a week and the omega-3 fatty acids will reduce your risk of heart disease. Make extra portions of fish for a luscious cold lunch. Add a chopped hard-boiled egg, yogurt or mayo, and dill or parsley, and you are close to meeting your daily nutritional requirements.

Convenient tuna pouches make another easy and nutritious fish lunch.

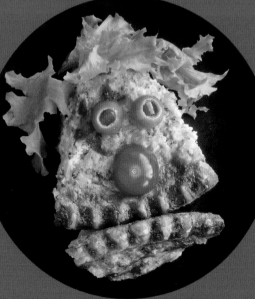

Pizza and Quiche Leftovers

A leftover slice of pizza or quiche topped with nutritious fixings packs a lunch full of vitamins and nutrients. Add a red pepper as a nose or a mouth and you'll add 300 percent of your daily vitamin intake!

Saladia

Lettuce, cucumber, blueberries, carrot, tomato, string beans

Flamenco

Melon, lettuce, pomegranate seeds, pineapple, strawberry

141

Beetnik *Lettuce, beets, red pepper, mushrooms, olives, cucumber, pickle*

Lettuceo
Lettuce, tomato, avocado, olives

V
A
R
I
A
T
I
O
N
S

Romaine-tic *Lettuce, cucumber, crackers, yogurt, olives, parsley, tomatoes, carrot, red pepper*

Tropicano *Lettuce, melon, strawberry, pineapple, walnuts, blueberries*

SALAD • LETTUCE • TOMATO • PEPPER • BROCCOLI • AVOCADO • CARROT • CUCUMBER • MUSHROOM • ARUGULA • BEET • SPINACH • FRUIT • RADISH • OLIVE • SNAP PEA • ASPARAGUS •

"Let your imagination run wild to make spontaneous food creations . . .

. . . with an artist's palette consisting of whatever healthy food is on hand."

144

Chickpeas: Petite and Powerful

Chickpeas (garbanzo beans) are legumes valued for their fiber content and great for digestion. They are also rich in anti-oxidants and even a one-third cup serving of chickpeas each day improves the body's control of blood sugar and insulin secretion. Hummus, made from chickpeas, is a good source of protein that can help lower cholesterol.

Make your own hummus or look for brands that are low in sodium.

Hummushy
Pita, hummus, cucumber, olives, carrot, radish, parsley

Happy Hummus

English muffin, hummus, olives, tomato, carrot, lettuce, celery

Tortillo

*Tortilla, hard-boiled egg, olives, chicken,
red pepper, cucumber, arugula*

146

Hold the Mayo

Mayonnaise is often used to make tuna salad, egg salad, and chicken salad. I mostly use plain nonfat yogurt or tzatziki on our salad sandwiches. At 70 to 100 calories a tablespoon, mayo has more than double the calories, the sodium, and the fat content. The one plus is that the fat in mayo helps absorb fat-soluble vitamins—A, D, E, and K.

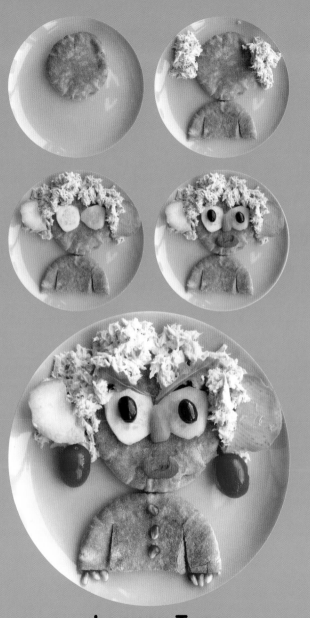

Looney Tuna

Pita, tuna salad, cucumber, olives, red pepper, carrot, grape tomatoes, pomegranate seeds, arugula

Guacamoleye

Pita, cucumber, garbanzo beans, guacamole, olives, carrot, tomato, chicken salad, parsley

Eggbert

Bread, cucumber, olives, tomato,
cheese, lettuce, egg salad

Topsy Tuna

Tuna salad, English muffin,
strawberry, cheese

Peas are not only known as a nutritional powerhouse, but also can be beaks, eyes, teeth, and buttons.

Broccoli keeps your blood strong and prevents anemia. It also works to clean your body of unwanted contaminants, and is a good source of vitamins D, A, and K.

Pea Hen

Chicken salad, snap peas, lettuce, broccoli, cucumber

Uncanny Canned Tuna

A can of tuna fish is a convenient way to meet the recommended intake of fish. It serves as a complete protein, and is a good source of omega-3 fatty acids. Make a whacky dish and watch your kids devour a nourishing meal: whole-grain bread, olives, tuna, healthy oil (like olive), tomato, cucumber, and parsley. What kid could turn this down?

Sweetie Potato

Sweet potato, grape tomato, olives, arugula, apple

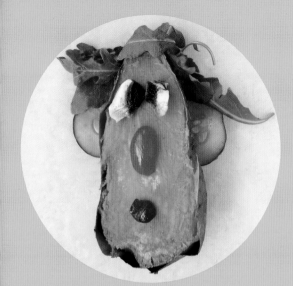

Yam Yum *Sweet potato, arugula, grape tomato, mushrooms, cucumber, cranberry*

Sweet Sweet Potatoes

Sweet potatoes are bursting with vitamins C and D and minerals. They contain iron for red and white cell production, and magnesium, which helps relieve stress.

Yammy *Sweet potato, arugula, radish, mushroom, Brussels sprouts, olives*

Glam Yam
Sweet potato, olives, arugula, fish, snap peas

Pasta People

Whole-wheat and multigrain pasta gives you energy, as well as some essential nutrients, including fiber, vitamins, magnesium, iron, and minerals. Pasta is versatile: it comes

in many shapes and sizes. It is inexpensive and a fantastic foundation for building a healthy meal. Pasta is great for a small dish, a hot lunch, or a cold salad. Most kids like pasta. Add some veggies or protein and increase the nutritional value. Rice also has a high-nutrient value.

Grow basil in a pot and make fresh pesto. It is delicious over pasta.

Mozzarelli

Mozzarella, olives, tomato, spaghetti, basil

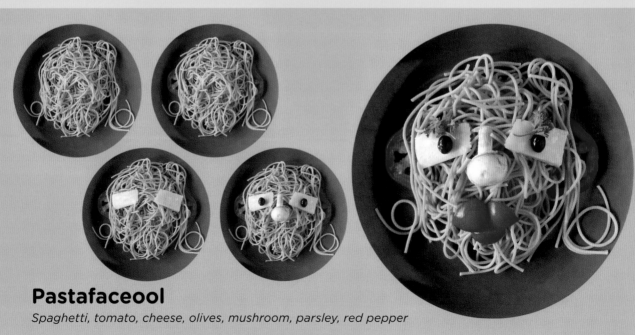

Pastafaceool

Spaghetti, tomato, cheese, olives, mushroom, parsley, red pepper

156

Legumes and Grains

Legumes are a variety of vegetables that include peas, lentils, split peas, lima beans, kidney beans, and garbanzo beans. They are low-fat sources of protein, vitamins, minerals, antioxidants, and dietary fiber. You feel full after eating a small amount. They are an ideal meat substitute and are cholesterol free. Legumes and whole grains go together to make a complete protein; when eaten together, they contain all nine essential amino acids.

Señor Rice

Rice, black beans, tomato, olives, parsley, red pepper

Silly Chili

Chili, cheese, olives, red pepper, carrot, cucumber, arugula

Oops Soup

*Bean soup, crackers, breadsticks,
red pepper, cheese, olives*

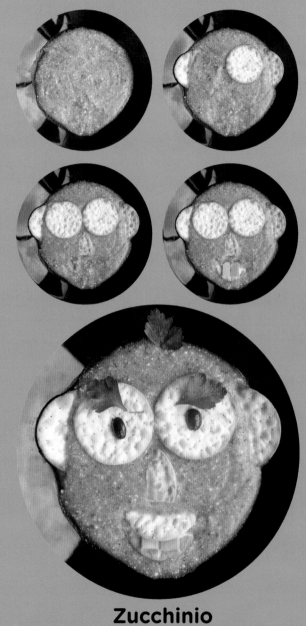

Zucchinio

*Zucchini soup, crackers, cheese,
parsley, olives*

159

Souped-Up Soup

There's nothing like the aroma of soup simmering on the stove. It's easy to make a hearty soup; it's a no-fuss comfort food, and what an effective way to use wilting vegetables! Don't forget to check the freezer for leftover grains and legumes and add them to the soup. Use your imagination, and you'll have a meal that's bursting with nutrients. Serve the soup one day with chunks of vegetables and puree the next day for a new meal. Or, bring the soup to the table along with extra fixings (shredded cheese, leftover chicken, whole-wheat tortilla chips), and let the family choose. Cold soups are a treat on a hot day. Simmer cut-up heads of broccoli or about three sliced zucchinis in broth and puree when the vegetables are soft. Mix in a cup of nonfat yogurt and chill. The bowl will be brimming with vitamins, protein, and calcium, and your family will lick it clean.

The word comes from the French "soupe."

161

Nutrition

CLEMENTINES MAKE **COOL** REDHEADS, SPIFFY SHOES, AND **MARVELOUS** MOUTHS. • STRING CHEESE ADDS LIMBER LIMBS TO A **WACKY** SNACK. • WHOLE-WHEAT PITA MAKES **PERFECT** PEOPLE. •

THE SKINNY ON NUTRITION

You start the day on empty, but don't run on empty.
After fasting all night, your body may start to use muscle tissue for
fuel if you don't refill the protein.

• • •

All calories are not equal. Empty calories (soda, cookies, solid fats)
add to your calorie intake, but have very little or no nutritional value.

• • •

Complex carbohydrates like popcorn, whole-grain cereals,
bread, and crackers are digested slowly and keep you
full for a long time.

Changing Habits

Changing eating habits doesn't have to be overwhelming. Start with small, manageable changes. Studies show that people who make small changes they can actually maintain do better than people who make drastic changes they can't stick with. If you feel good about making one change, you are more amenable to make another. And another.

A recent *New York Times* article reported on parents who are in denial about their children's obesity issues. More than half of the parents of obese preschool children described their children as "about the right weight."

Parents are partially in denial because they worry that it's too much work to change eating habits. They worry about becoming the "food police" at home. They worry that they will have to eat differently too. Even though they are putting their children's health at risk, their coping mechanism is denial.

To change a habit, pinpoint the trigger. What makes you grab cookies instead of fruit? Is it the time of day, your mood, or the situation? Habits are often automatic.

But changing eating habits and encouraging healthy attitudes toward food doesn't have to be difficult. It takes only six weeks to form new habits. The first step is for the family to approach the issue together. Often the child is being teased at school and the parents don't even know. The kids want help, but don't know what to do.

One simple change is to serve water instead of juice or soda. That one change cuts down on almost half the calories in an average kid's diet. Just one sweetened 12-ounce soda adds up to 250 calories. A 12-ounce fruit drink adds at least 215 calories.

There are other benefits to drinking water: the added water fills you up and you eat less. Sometimes you think you're hungry, but you're really thirsty and don't realize it. Drink water and it will satisfy your imagined hunger.

When your body doesn't have enough water, body functions slow down to conserve energy. Drinking water also revs up your metabolism. Plus, drinking water instead of sweetened drinks saves money.

Once drinking water has become a new habit, begin to buy cereals without added sugar. Fresh fruit is a natural sweetener. It also has vitamins, minerals, and fiber that are great for your digestion. Use fruit on pancakes instead of syrup. Sugar and syrup add empty calories, but fruit provides a wide variety of nutrients.

Want another easy change? How about moving five more minutes each day? By the end of the week, that will add up to 35 minutes.

You could also try this: As a family, take time to make a silly, healthy meal together. Slow down and look at your food—smell it, touch it, and enjoy it visually. Make it a family project on a weekend morning. The creative experience will give everyone pleasure and create a positive emotional connection with nourishing food. Slowing down and taking the time to make something fun together also prevents you from wolfing down food so fast that your brain never gets the chance to register that you have eaten.

POWERFUL PROTEIN

Eat a high-protein meal at breakfast to reduce hunger all day. Protein is filling and satisfying. Keep it lean. Avoid fatty meats and full-fat dairy. Good lean proteins are fish, lean turkey, chicken, lean meats, eggs, low-fat dairy, and beans.

Protein is used to make hair, nails, skin, muscle, and cells. The body needs protein for optimal brain function. It also needs protein to build and repair tissues and it's a building block of bones, cartilage, and blood. After a rigorous workout, bodybuilders eat protein to rebuild and repair muscle. The body does not store protein, so there is no spare protein to use when the body needs a new supply. You need a fresh supply of low-fat protein daily. Studies show that dieters who increase their protein intake to 30 percent eat 450 fewer calories a day.

Eggs: An egg is inexpensive and has one of the highest-quality proteins found in any food. Only 70 calories, it also has lots of vitamins and minerals. If you eat a well-balanced low-fat diet, then eggs do not have a negative impact on cholesterol.

Nuts: Nuts are packed with protein, fiber, vitamin E, and tons of vitamins and minerals. Nuts are little nuggets of nutrition and energy. Eating a handful can help lower cholesterol and the risk of heart disease. The fat, fiber, and protein in nuts are filling, so a small amount can make you feel satisfied.

Seeds: When you want to reach for an unhealthy food, take a few handfuls of sunflower seeds or any other kind of seed. The fat in seeds helps you absorb nutrients in vegetables eaten at the same meal.

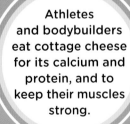

Peanut Butter: Peanut butter is rich in protein, niacin, and folate. A favorite for kids, peanut butter is a healthy way to start the day and also a good snack.

Cottage Cheese: Cottage cheese—the name is said to have originated when people made it in their cottages from milk left over from making butter—is both a dairy and a protein. Low in fat and nutritious, it is an easy breakfast. Add a little cinnamon (a good source of vitamin K, iron, dietary fiber, calcium, and manganese) and it keeps you satisfied for hours. Cottage cheese is also good with fruit.

Athletes and bodybuilders eat cottage cheese for its calcium and protein, and to keep their muscles strong.

VITAL VEGGIES

It's hard to get kids to eat salad and vegetables. Entice the kids with salad greens and other vegetables by mixing them with foods kids really like.

Try adding fruit to your salad. A juicy piece of watermelon or a slice of orange makes a salad hard to resist. Nuts, dried cranberries, and cheese are other goodies that children may enjoy in a salad. Rummage through the refrigerator—a sliced cooked potato, cooked rice, or leftover grains might delight your child.

Salads can easily be made to look like faces. Additionally, dark, leafy greens make great hair on faces that you design with other healthy ingredients.

Dark Leafy Greens: Greens add fanciful touches to edible food images. They are filled with vitamins, minerals, and the calcium needed to become strong and healthy.

Peppers: Red peppers are low in calories and saturated fats and are a good source of vitamins K, C, A, E, B6, and magnesium. Red and yellow peppers have more vitamin C and A than green peppers. The collagen from the vitamin C in red peppers is great for the skin. Tell that to your teenager and you may have a run on peppers! Red peppers also support night vision. They are a great superfood. Pepper rings also make great hula hoops for your funny food!

Carrots: Carrots are rich in the antioxidants that keep us from getting sick. They are rich in vitamins A and K. Did you know that carrots come in many colors—purple, yellow, and red? The colors come from the different antioxidants. If you eat two or three pounds of carrots a week, the palms of your hands or skin might turn orange. Don't worry; they'll turn back to their normal color when you stop eating so many carrots! Carrots are great raw and make a great carrier for a dip. They are also a great addition to an artist's palette. They can be cut to make limbs, lips, and even buttons. Sliced or curled carrots make ridiculous redheads.

Spaghetti Squash: This is an amazing vegetable: when cooked, the inside flesh separates to form spaghetti-like strands. It fills you up and has only a few calories. It can substitute for spaghetti if you are counting calories. The fiber forms a gel in your digestive tract that helps remove cholesterol from your body. Spaghetti squash contains minerals and several B vitamins, as well as C, E, and K. It's fun to scrape the squash and watch the flesh turn into strands. Plus, spaghetti squash makes hilarious hair!

Eat Your Colors

Each color of fruit and vegetable has its own unique set
of vitamins and minerals to keep you in good health.
They keep you from getting sick, build strong bodies,
and support good health. Eat them
as part of your breakfast,
lunch, or snack.

172

"One simple golden rule for parents: as long as the plate is half full of fruits and vegetables, and paired with lean protein, whole grains, and low-fat dairy, we're golden." —MICHELLE OBAMA

173

FABULOUS FRUIT

Fabulous fruits are delicious any time of day. They sweeten any meal and help you meet your daily requirements of vitamins and minerals. They are yummy fresh, dried, frozen, or canned (without added sugar). Fruits make good grab-and-go snacks and are much healthier than scarfing down a sugary drink or snack.

Apples: Full of calcium and iron, apples help you from getting cavities. (But you still need to brush your teeth.) Apples are also great if you have an upset stomach. Don't skip the peel—nearly half of the vitamin C found in an apple is located in the flesh just beneath the skin, which contains valuable amounts of insoluble fiber.

Berries: Blueberries, raspberries, strawberries, and blackberries are some of the highest antioxidant foods available. Antioxidants are like sponges that clean up the things that your body doesn't need. They prevent your body from getting diseases. Eat a variety of berries for breakfast, lunch, and snacks.

• Strawberries have more vitamin C than oranges. One cup of strawberries has 160 percent of the recommended daily dose of vitamin C.

Did you know that every strawberry has about 200 seeds and they are on the outside of the fruit?

• Blueberries are great for your brain. They help it work better. They are also a good source of vitamin K, which keeps your bones strong.

Oranges: Oranges are juicy and quench your thirst. They are a good source of potassium and vitamins A, B, and C. Oranges also help your body fight diseases. The pectin in oranges helps your body attack cholesterol in your intestines and helps regulate blood glucose levels. The pectin is like a sponge that wipes away toxins, such as lead or mercury, from your body.

Clementines are loaded with vitamins, minerals, and other nutrients— good for your muscles. Clementines are easy to peel and small enough to carry in a purse.

Kiwis: Packing as much vitamin C as an orange, kiwis come from California and New Zealand. They have a unique sweet taste. In addition to being an exotic fruit in your salad or cereal, kiwis contain many vitamins and minerals that promote your health, and the black seeds provide essential nutrients. Eating a couple of kiwis a day can reduce the chances of a blood clot. Kiwis also make spectacular eyes and ears for funny food!

GLORIOUS GRAINS

Whole grains are a great source of vitamins, magnesium, iron, and fiber, and are a natural aid to healthy digestion. Whole-grain pasta and rice offer a high nutrient value.

Refined grains are processed—the bran and the germ is taken away, as well as some of the nutrients you need. White flour, white rice, and white bread are examples of refined-grain products.

Grains are an important part of a balanced diet. They give you energy and help your brain and nervous system work well. Complex carbohydrates are digested slowly and give the body lasting energy levels. Oatmeal, popcorn, whole-grain cereals, breads, and crackers are all healthy grains.

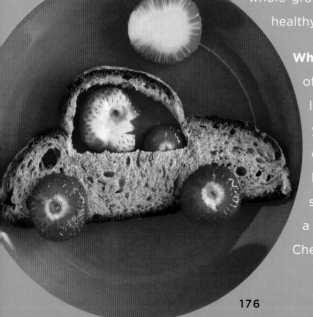

Whole-Grain Cereals: These are a good source of soluble fiber, which acts almost like a little sponge, sucking up bad cholesterol in your body. Look for healthy options and read the labels. Many healthy-sounding names have a high sugar content. Check for 100 percent

Whole grains take longer to cook than refined grains. Cook several portions at once and freeze or refrigerate for other meals.

whole grain, with at least three grams of fiber and two grams or less of sugar. The other ingredients on the list should be recognizable. Introduce a new healthier cereal to your family in a playful way. Make a funny image with it. There's a chance your kid will start munching on the cereal as he or she uses it for hair. Hint: when introducing a new cereal, pair it with something you know your kid likes—a banana, some almonds, or raisins.

Whole-Grain Breads: Choosing whole-grain bread can be confusing. If whole grain is not listed as the first or second ingredient, it is not whole-grain bread. Even if it is brown and has wheat or multigrain on the label, it is not necessarily a whole-grain loaf. Look for products that have a yellow Whole Grain Stamp. Whole grains lower the risk of many chronic diseases, including coronary heart disease, stroke, colorectal cancer, and type 2 diabetes. Think whole grain when buying any wheat product: crackers, bagels, muffins, tortillas, waffles, pitas, and pizzas.

DYNAMIC DAIRY

Eating dairy increases the intake of calcium that prevents osteoporosis and makes your muscles and bones strong. Dairy products provide essential nutrients, vitamins, protein, and potassium—all part of a healthy diet.

Yogurt: It's great for breakfast with fruit and cinnamon or flaxseed. It's delicious in pancake batter if you use less baking powder. It's a great snack or dessert with some nuts and honey. A favorite is homemade zucchini soup mixed with a cup of yogurt. Try tzatziki, a Greek dish made with drained yogurt, cucumbers, garlic, and a little olive oil. Try it with carrot or cucumber slices or whole-wheat pita bread. Eating yogurt keeps your colon clean. It has bacterial cultures that replenish the bacteria lost when taking antibiotics. It also has a good balance of proteins, fats, carbohydrates, and minerals.

Cheese: Cheese is often thought of as a fatty food product, but it has many health benefits. Choose from the variety of cheeses available at the cheese counter of your market. Eat cheese in a salad, for a snack, or as an elegant end to a meal. Eating cheese after a meal helps prevent tooth decay. It has properties that can also prevent cancer. Did you know that cheese enhances your good looks? The vitamin B in cheese is great for maintaining

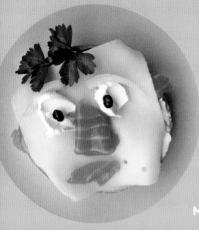

supple healthy skin, and the calcium helps give you shiny hair and strong nails. The tryptophan in cheese also helps lower stress and reduces insomnia.

Milk: Milk is an affordable source of many essential nutrients: calcium, vitamin D, and potassium. It is especially important for growing kids, who need to build strong bones. Milk comes in a variety of types: whole, reduced fat (2%), low fat (1%), fat free, organic, and lactose free. All milks contain the nine essential nutrients found in whole milk but some have less fat.

Individually wrapped part-skim cheeses are healthy proteins and easy to carry. Add a fruit and whole-wheat cracker to the cheese and you've got an excellent nutrient-rich snack.

ire's Eating History: What you eat reflects your family traditions. My immigrant parents ught their food habits with them. Good: whole-grain bread and vegetables. Bad: cheap fatty at and chicken fat. Our lives changed when my mother took free nutrition classes at the Henry eet Settlement House. She was proud to teach us what she had learned: not to peel potatoes ore cooking; the skin of an apple had more value than the inside; raw vegetables make great cks; and the importance of a healthy breakfast.

Now, three generations later, those eating habits are ply embedded in our family and those of my siblings. amily gatherings, raw veggies are a staple and re's never any leftover salad. Knowing that a ily's eating habits can change inspired us to nk we could make a difference, so we began ny food workshops in schools.

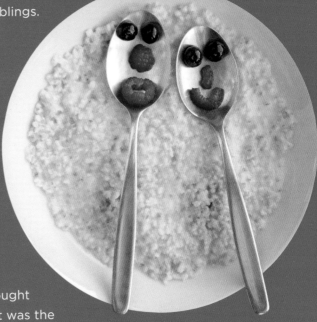

's Eating History: When I met Bill, his idea breakfast was a brownie and a soda—if he at at all. One morning, while running to catch ain, he almost fainted. A caring police officer with him on the subway platform, bought something to eat, and lectured him about the ortance of eating breakfast. Bill watched me bling salad and vegetables with gusto and thought enjoyed them so much he would try them. That was the inning of our family's tradition of healthy eating.

ople are more likely to develop healthy behaviors if a partner is also changing eating habits."
JAMA Internal Medicine, January 19, 2015

Keep Playing!